D0535649

COLLECTING DATA

Daily temperature data

Mon.	Tue.	Wed.	Thu.	Fri.	Sat.	Sun.
82°F	80°F	85°F	91°F	84°F	86°F	86°F

Daily temperature line plot

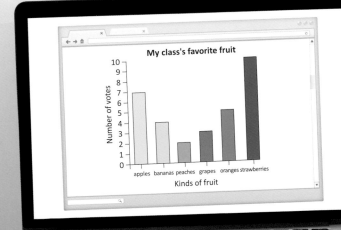

Which of these fruits do you like the best?

☐ apples
☐ bananas
☒ peaches
☐ grapes
☐ oranges
☐ strawberries

My class's favorite fruit

Lizann Flatt

Crabtree Publishing Company

www.crabtreebooks.com

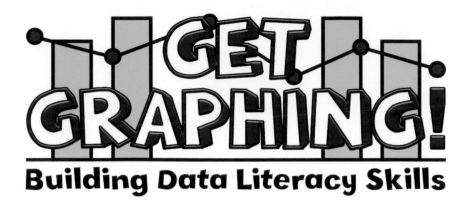

Building Data Literacy Skills

Author: Lizann Flatt

Series research and development:
Reagan Miller

Substantive editor: Crystal Sikkens

Editorial director: Kathy Middleton

Photo research: Crystal Sikkens,
Katherine Berti

Design: Katherine Berti

Proofreader and indexer:
Petrice Custance

Print and production coordinator:
Katherine Berti

Image credits:
All images by Shutterstock

Library and Archives Canada Cataloguing in Publication

Flatt, Lizann, author
          Collecting data / Lizann Flatt.

(Get graphing! Building data literacy skills)
Includes index.
Issued in print and electronic formats.
ISBN 978-0-7787-2633-3 (hardback).--
ISBN 978-0-7787-2637-1 (paperback).--
ISBN 978-1-4271-1840-0 (html)

          1. Science--Methodology--Juvenile literature. 2. Observation
(Scientific method)--Juvenile literature. 3. Mathematical statistics--
Juvenile literature. 4. Quantitative research--Juvenile literature.
I. Title.

Q175.2.F53 2016   j507.2   C2016-903321-X
                                                          C2016-903322-8

Library of Congress Cataloging-in-Publication Data

CIP available at the Library of Congress

Crabtree Publishing Company

www.crabtreebooks.com   1-800-387-7650

Printed in Canada/072016/EF20160630

Published in Canada
Crabtree Publishing
616 Welland Ave.
St. Catharines, Ontario
L2M 5V6

Published in the United States
Crabtree Publishing
PMB 59051
350 Fifth Avenue, 59th Floor
New York, New York 10118

Published in the United Kingdom
Crabtree Publishing
Maritime House
Basin Road North, Hove
BN41 1WR

Published in Australia
Crabtree Publishing
3 Charles Street
Coburg North
VIC 3058

Contents

Questions and Answers

People are always looking for answers to questions. Some questions have already been answered and the information can be found in books, magazines, newspapers, or on the Internet. Information collected about people or things is called **data**. Data is shared through words, numbers, and drawings. Some drawings are in the form of a **chart** or **graph**. Graphs and charts show data using lines, shapes, and colors.

How many minutes did Juan spend reading each day this week? This line graph uses dots and lines to show the answer.

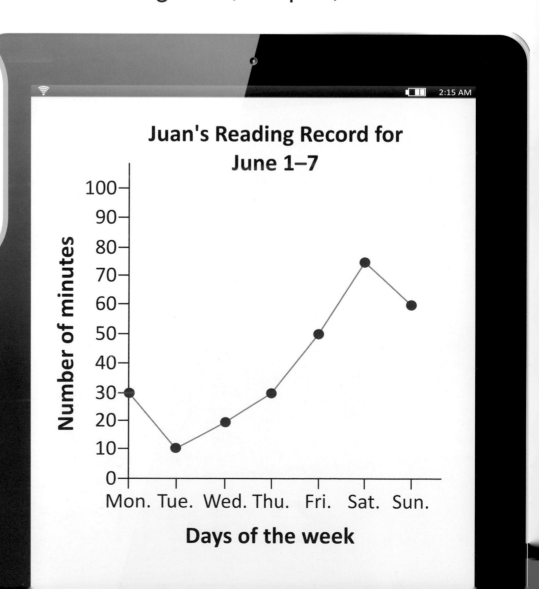

Finding Answers

Sometimes you cannot find the answers you are looking for in books or on the Internet. You might have to **collect**, or gather, data yourself to get an answer to your question.

This girl wants to know how many students in her class walk to school and how many take the bus. Can she find the answer by looking on the Internet?

Steps for Data Collecting

It is best to create a plan before you begin collecting data. Following the three simple steps below will help to make sure you collect the data you need to answer your question properly.

Steps for collecting data:

1. *Pick a topic and come up with a question.*

2. *Decide how you will gather your data.*

3. *Choose the best way to organize and record your data so you can use it to answer your question.*

Determining Your Question

Data collecting begins with a question you want answered. Some questions can be answered simply with a yes or a no. Other questions have several possible answers. The question you ask needs to be created carefully so that it will give you the answer or the information you need. Before creating your question, think about what you want to find out, and what kind of data you need to gather in order to answer your question.

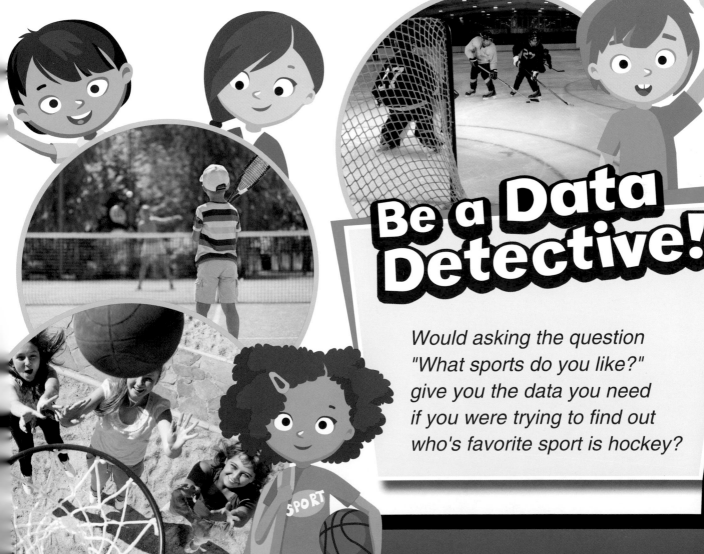

Be a Data Detective!

Would asking the question "What sports do you like?" give you the data you need if you were trying to find out who's favorite sport is hockey?

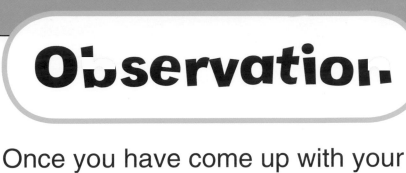

Observation

Once you have come up with your question, it's time to collect your data. There are different ways to collect the data you need to answer your questions. Gathering data using your **senses** is known as observation. Observation is one way to collect data. It helps you sort, or group things, based on the way they look, feel, taste, sound, or smell.

How are these blocks alike? How are they different? You can use your sense of sight to sort these blocks by color.

Sorting and Counting

Once you have sorted objects using your senses, you can then use them to answer questions. For some questions you might need to observe and sort objects, and then count them to collect your data.

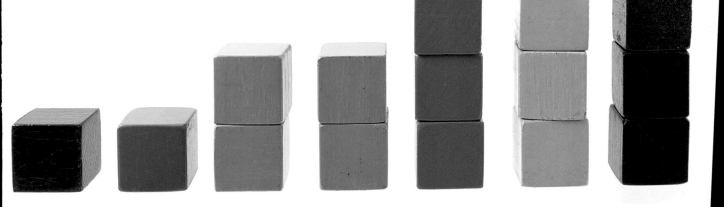

Be a Data Detective!

Answer these questions using the sorted blocks above.

1. How many blocks are yellow?

2. What is the total number of red and green blocks?

Tests and Experiments

Some questions cannot be answered by only using observation. One example is if you want to know which objects will a magnet pull, or **attract**. To find the answer to this question, you need to do an **experiment** to collect your data. An experiment is a test done to find out something.

One way to test which objects a magnet will attract is to hold each object to the magnet and see which ones are pulled to it.

Creating a Test

Max's teacher gave each student a pencil, an eraser, a ball, and a calculator. Then she asked the class, "Which of these objects will roll?" Max knew he would have to do an experiment to find the answer to this question. He used a book to make a ramp and then, one at a time, placed each object at the top of the ramp and let it go. Max was able to observe which of the objects rolled down the book.

By doing a test, Max collected the data he needed to answer his teacher's question. The objects that rolled were the pencil and the ball.

Measurement

If you wanted to find out which of your friends was the tallest you could stand them all next to one another and use your sense of sight to observe who was taller. However, if you wanted to find out the exact height of your tallest friend, you would have to measure him or her. Measuring is another way to collect data.

*Measurements can be recorded in different **units** depending on what you are measuring. Length, height, and width is often measured in centimeters, inches, or feet.*

Measuring Temperature

Aaron measured the temperature outside for seven days to see which day was the hottest. Temperature is measured in degrees Farenheit or Celsius. He **recorded** his data in the chart below.

Be a Data Detective!

Answer the questions below using Aaron's data.

1. Which day of the week was the hottest?

2. What is the difference between the hottest day and the coolest day?

Daily temperature

Mon.	Tue.	Wed.	Thu.	Fri.	Sat.	Sun.
82°F	80°F	85°F	91°F	84°F	86°F	86°F

Polls and Surveys

Taking a **poll** or **survey** is another way to gather the data you need to answer your question. When you take a poll, you ask a number of people a question. A survey is like a poll, but it includes several questions. You then count how many people give a specific answer. Each answer in a poll or survey is called a vote.

Data in this poll is collected by counting the number of raised hands.

Accurate Data

When doing a poll or survey, it is important to get an answer from as many people as possible to make sure your data is **accurate**, or correct. For example, Jenna wants to bring one kind of fruit to school as a treat for her classmates. She plans to use her poll to learn which fruit the highest number of her classmates would like best. She must include as many classmates as possible in her poll. Only asking one or two classmates will not give Jenna the data she needs.

Which of these fruits do you like the best?

☐ apples

☐ bananas

☒ peaches

☐ grapes

☐ oranges

☐ strawberries

Polls and surveys can be given in person, online, or on paper, like the one above.

15

Organizing the Data

How you organize and record your data is important. You want your data to be clear and easy to read so you can make sense of the data you have collected. It is also important to clearly show your data if you are sharing it with others.

Emma's plant height data

5 cm

9 cm

10 cm

7   12

13 cm

14 cm

16

Different Ways

You can organize your data in a number of ways. Some data can be recorded on a checklist or chart, such as Aaron's data chart on page 13. Other data, such as from a poll or survey, is often easiest to read if it is recorded on a **tally chart**, **Venn diagram**, or **line plot**.

Be a Data Detective!

The students in Mrs. Wilson's grade 2 class were given seeds to plant. They then observed their plant's growth and recorded its height from Day 7 to 14. Emma's and Jacob's collected data are shown below on pages 16 and 17. Which data results are easiest to read? Why?

Jacob's plant height data

Measurements of plant height from day 7 to day 14

Days	Measurements in cm
Day 7	5
Day 8	7
Day 9	9
Day 10	10
Day 11	12
Day 12	13
Day 13	14
Day 14	16

Tally Charts

Tally charts can be a great way to organize data, especially when taking a poll or survey. A tally chart is a table that uses **tally marks** to show data. When Jenna collected the papers from her poll (shown on page 15), she made a tally mark on her tally chart in the row that matched each vote.

Jenna put the tally marks in groups of 5 to make them easier to count.

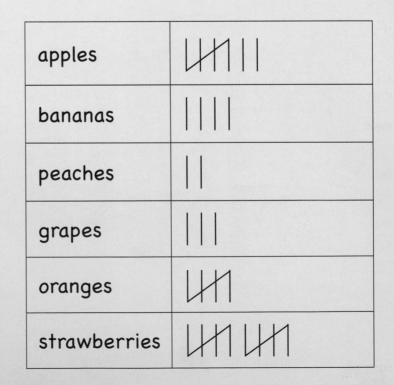

Which of these fruits do you like the best?

apples								
bananas					
peaches			
grapes				
oranges						
strawberries											

Data on Graphs

The data on a tally chart can be put on a graph to make it easier for people to understand the information. The graph below is a bar graph. The top of each bar lines up with a number on the **y-axis**, or the line going straight up and down. This number shows the total number of votes for each fruit.

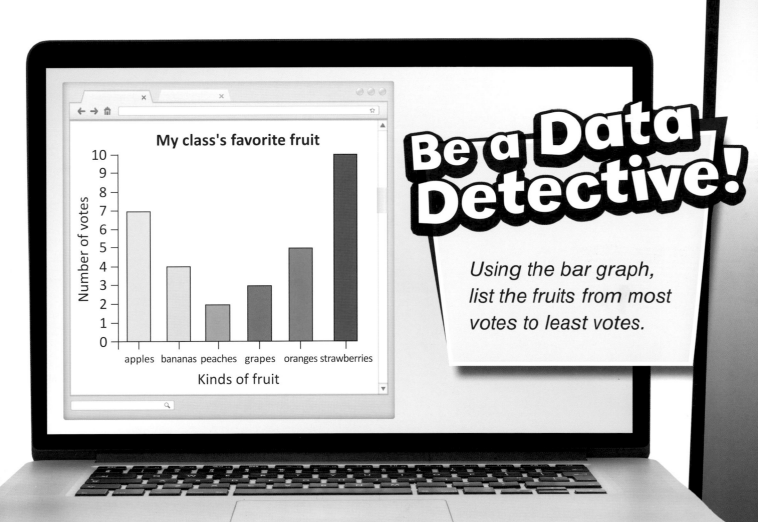

My class's favorite fruit

Number of votes

apples bananas peaches grapes oranges strawberries

Kinds of fruit

Be a Data Detective!

Using the bar graph, list the fruits from most votes to least votes.

By looking at the graph, which fruit do you think Jenna will be bringing to share with her classmates?

Venn Diagrams

Venn diagrams are another way you can sort and organize your data. A Venn diagram uses circles that overlap to show how things relate. Mrs. Kaur's grade 3 class has agreed to help with the school carnival. Mrs. Kaur hands each student a poll to fill out. The poll is to find out which students want to help at the bake sale, and which ones want to help at the garage sale.

Each student will write their name on the paper and then check off if they want to help with the bake sale, the garage sale, or both.

Showing the Data

Mrs. Kaur shows the data from her poll in the Venn diagram below. The names of the students that want to help with the bake sale are in the left circle. The names of the students that want to help with the garage sale are in the right circle. Students that are willing to help at both are shown in the middle.

Bake sale   Garage sale

Nathan

Brooklyn

Jayden

Ella

Jackson

Daniel

Zoe

Nathan

Kaitlyn

Donna

Ava

Chloe

Michelle

Maya

Stephanie

Line Plots

A line plot is a way of organizing data that shows measurements on a horizontal line. Aaron's temperature data from page 13 is shown on the line plot below. Each temperature in his chart is shown with an "X" above the matching number on the line plot.

Daily temperature data

Mon.	Tue.	Wed.	Thu.	Fri.	Sat.	Sun.
82°F	80°F	85°F	91°F	84°F	86°F	86°F

Daily temperature line plot

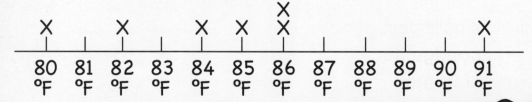

Be a Data Detective!

Katie measured each of her friends feet to see who's was the longest. The measurements were 16 cm, 17 cm, 17 cm, 19 cm, 20 cm, and 19 cm. Create a line plot using Katie's data.

Learning More

Books

Bader, Bonnie. *Family Reunion*. Penguin Young Readers, 2003.

Harris, Trudy. *Tally Cat Keeps Track*. Millbrook Press, 2010.

Leedy, Loreen. *The Great Graph Contest*. Holiday House, 2006.

Murphy, Stuart. *Tally O'Malley* (Math Start). Harper Collins Publishers, 2004.

Websites

Practice reading Venn diagrams here:
https://ca.ixl.com/math/grade-2/venn-diagrams-with-three-circles

Have fun with data collection here:
www.turtlediary.com/game/charts-and-graphing.html

Test your line plot skills here:
www.splashmath.com/math-skills/second-grade/data/read-data-from-line-plots

About the Author

Lizann Flatt has written many nonfiction books for children. You can find her online at www.lizannflatt.com

Get Graphing Online!

Organizing your data on graphs can be done both on paper and online. The link below features different websites that will create graphs based on the data you enter. Most websites let you print or save your graph when you are finished. You can begin by making different graphs using the data found in this book.

http://interactivesites. weebly.com/graphing.html

Glossary

Note: Some boldfaced words are defined where they appear in the text.

data Information that is gathered or collected

line plot A graph that displays data as points on a number line

recorded To write down information or data

senses The five ways to take in information (see, hear, taste, touch, and smell)

tally chart A way to show data using tally marks in a table

tally mark A vertical or diagonal line used for counting

Venn diagram A diagram that uses circles or other shapes to show how things are the same or different

Index

Answers

Page 4: Mon: 30, Tues: 10, Wed: 20, Thu: 30, Fri: 50, Sat: 75, Sun: 60

Page 5: No, she will need to ask her classmates the question herself

Page 7: No, a better question to ask would be "What is your favorite sport?"

Page 8: The books are all the same size, but they are different colors

Page 9: 1) 4; 2) 6

Page 13: 1) Thursday; 2)11°F

Page 17: Jacob's are easiest to read because they are neatly organized

Page 19: strawberries

Page 22: Saturday and Sunday